The Magic of Time

To Luke, Brody, Audrey, Emmy, Camilla, Helena, Theo, and more wee ones.

You have all you need inside of you.
Be patient with yourself, work hard,
and wait for good things to come.

ISBN: 979-8-9928394-0-1

Printed in the United States of America

Illustrated by Claudia Gadotti

First Edition 2025

Alonzo was **bold**,
he was **busy** and **bright**.

Exploring his world
filled his day and his night.

He chased bugs on a hunt
or swam in his pool.

September was here!
It is time to **start school!**

He jumped out of bed twenty minutes to eight,
And zoomed through
the doors fifteen minutes too late!

The children were seated with pencils in hand.
They turned to Alonzo to see him crash land!

Alonzo heard **giggles**; he wanted to cry.
The voice in his head hollered

"**Stand up and try!**"

He flew to the closet to hang up his coat,
Then promptly sat down with a lump in his throat.

At recess, the kids were all choosing their teams.
The playground was filled with loud yammers and screams.

He sloshed past the swings, past the slide and the bars.
Then Alonzo spied puddles as big as boxcars!

Alonzo's head **swiveled**
around like an owl.

All eyes turned to him.
With a piercing fierce howl

He **raced** through puddles
like speed boats that fly!

Then **slipped** on his belly,
his face in mud pie.

Completing his work seemed to take extra long.
He did some work right but then often was wrong.

And why was he always the last one who was done?
He feels more himself when he's outside and can run!

Alonzo's first year as he settled in school,
Was like a long train running fast out of fuel.

He started out strong but couldn't keep up.
He slowed and he slowed til he wouldn't speed up.

Time moves along; and a new school year was here.
Returning to school made Alonzo feel fear.

He tried to make friends when he went out to play.
But Alonzo was shy, so he left in dismay.

Alonzo was tired, his mind couldn't think.
He laid down his head, went to sleep in a wink.

The book on his desk hit his lap then the ground.
It landed like thunder and made a "clonk" sound.

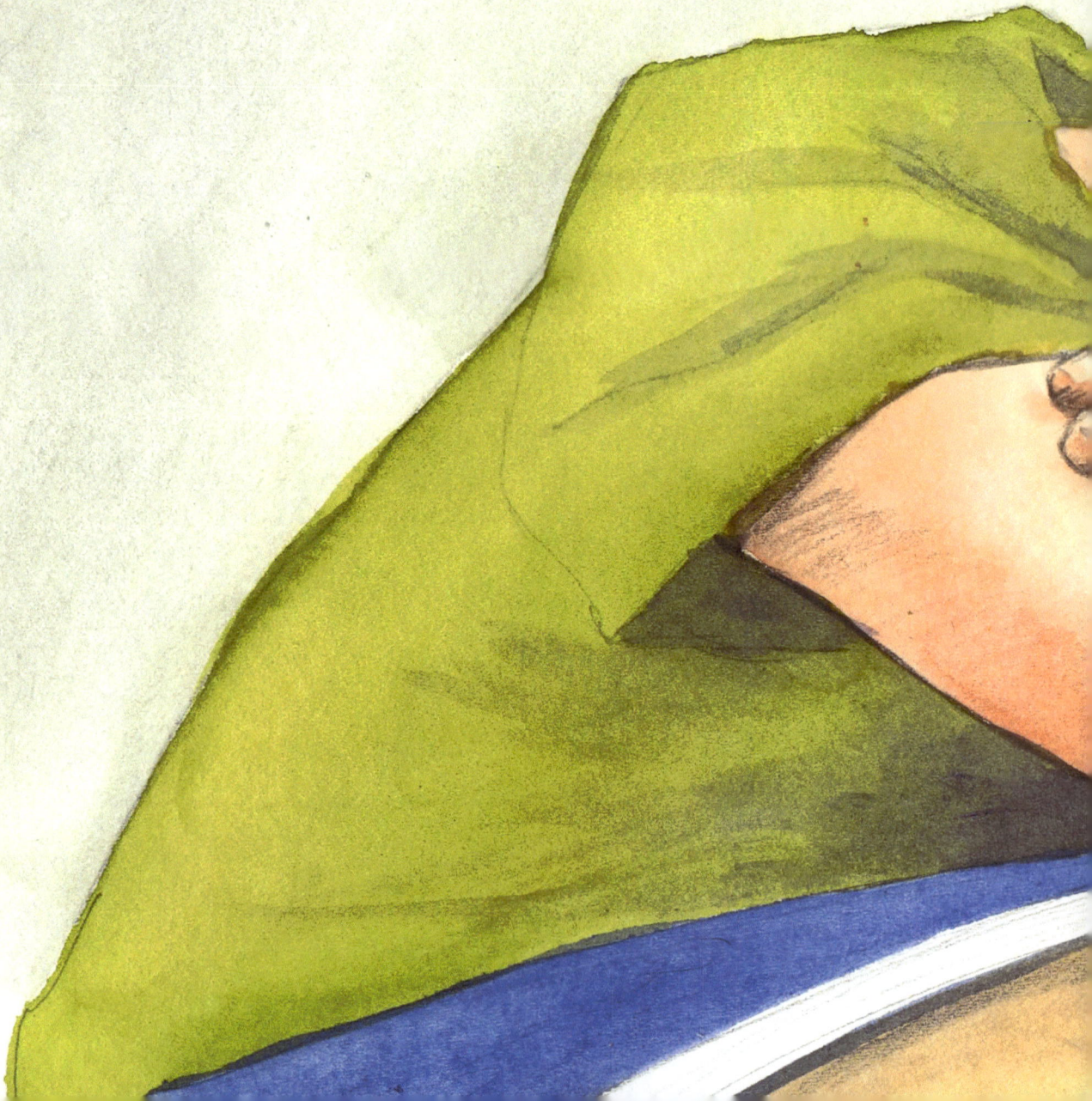

He **jerked** up his head,
almost fell off his chair.

He opened his eyes,
then he saw Miss McNair.

Her eyes were so **kind.**
With the **warmth** of her smile,

She put him at ease
when she walked down the aisle.

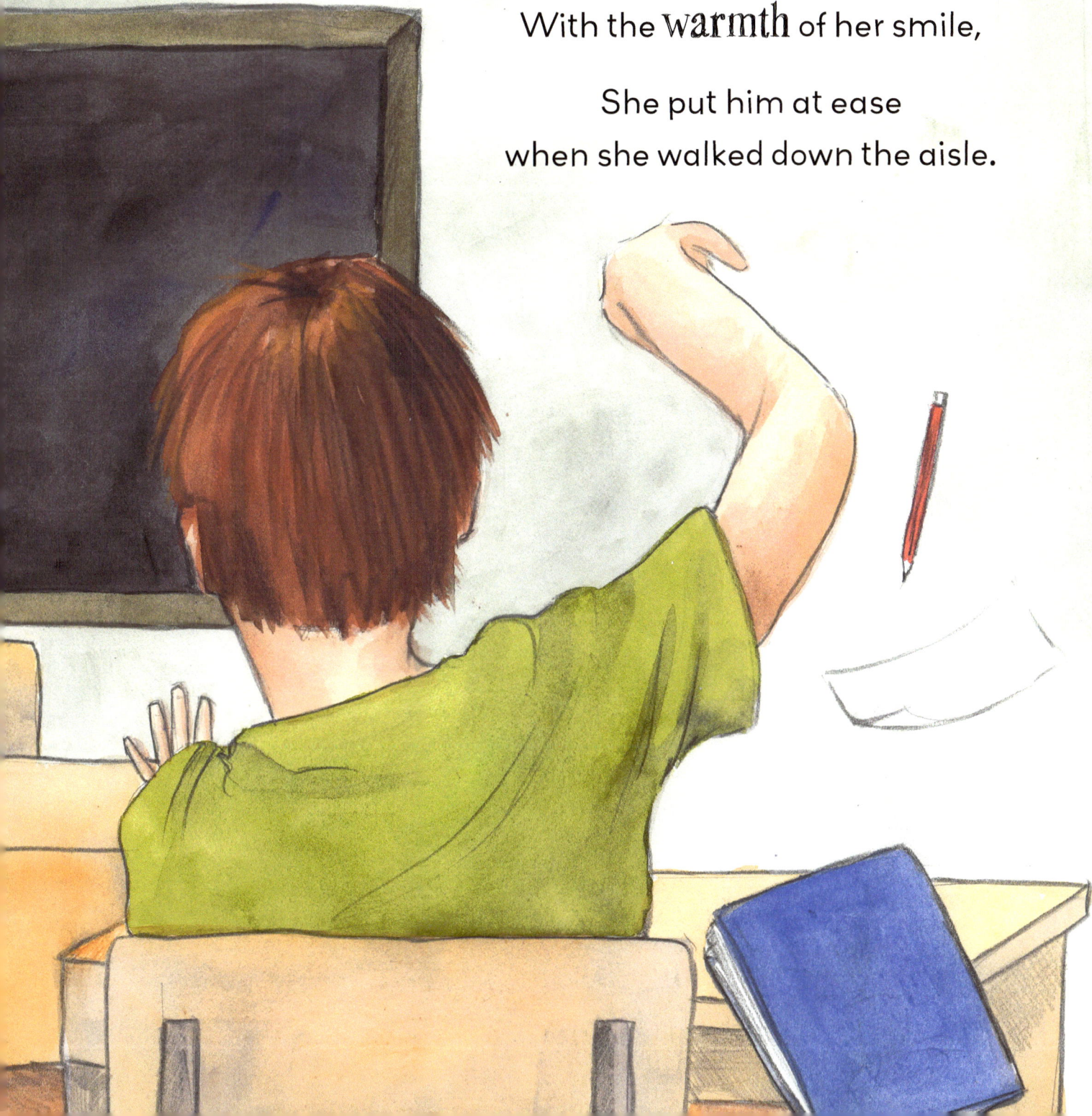

"Have **patience** my dear, it takes time to grow **strong**.
I know you are thinking, "It's taking too long!"

The change happens slowly with the Magic of Time
For now, on this day, you're a perfect design...

Keep looking forward, keep trying your best.
* **The Magic of Time** will do all the rest."

Alonzo is waiting for magic to start,
But hope of the "**Magic**" soon fled from his heart.

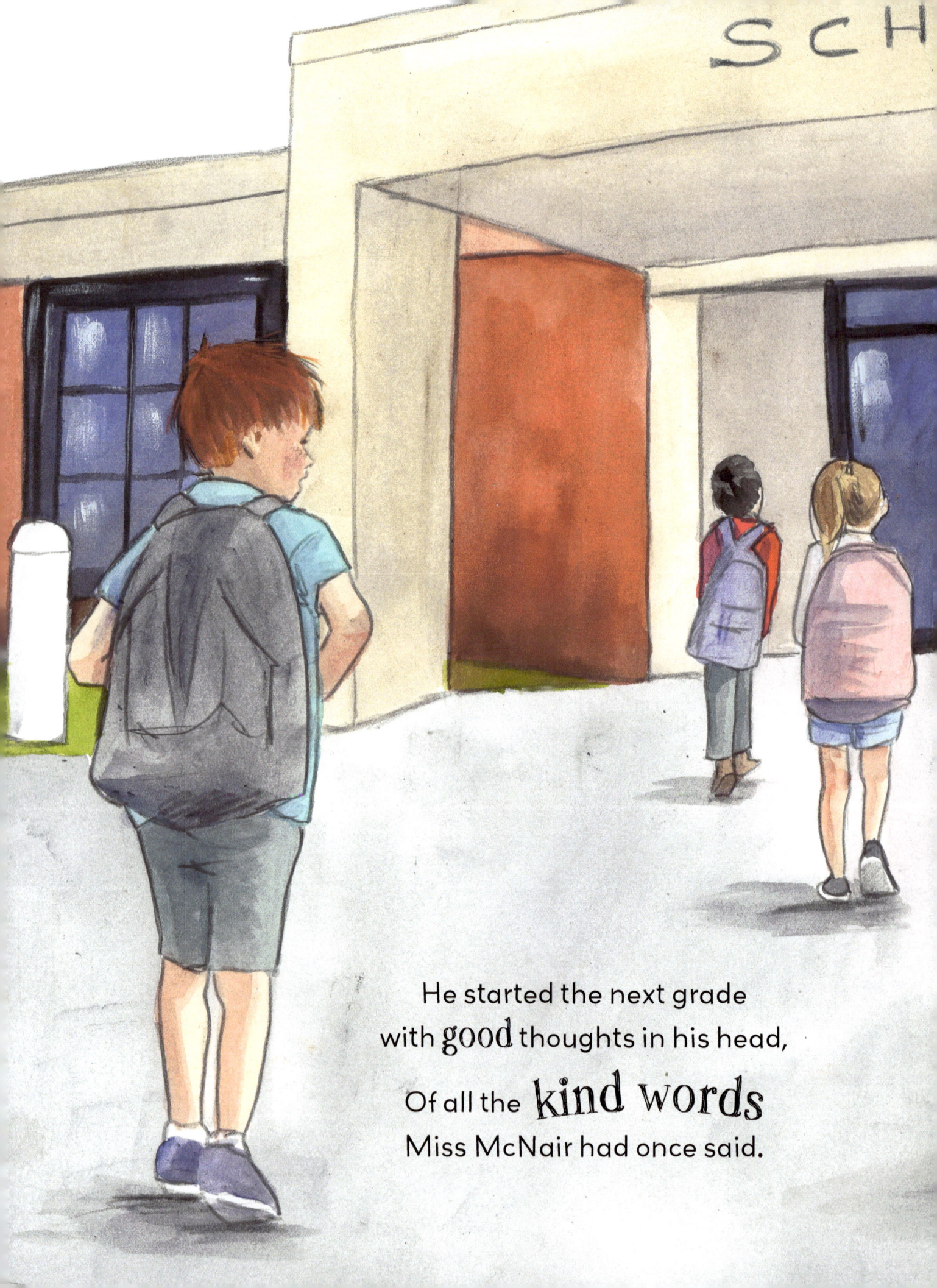

He started the next grade
with **good** thoughts in his head,

Of all the **kind words**
Miss McNair had once said.

"For just as I am, I'm a **perfect** *design*.
I learn my own way and in my own time."

Alonzo's new teacher whose name was Ms. Crockett,
Asked him about all the things in his pocket

The task was to write. He wrote less than he should.
The spelling was wrong, but the words were **all good**.

"The beach was a place to find rocks in the sand.
I found a smooth rock that had washed up on land.

A rock starts its life as a hot melted mess.
The pressure around it creates lots of stress.

This rock in my pocket was born long ago,
And shaped by the waves over time down below.

A rock can be buried down deep in the earth.
In time, it can turn into gems of great worth.

I found an old marble that lost all its gloss.
The porch kept it safe since the time it was tossed.

The marble I found there looks just like the moon…
A pearl swirled in dust as if stirred with a spoon.

I look to the sky at the moon and beyond
It's there every night as our time travels on.

It orbits the earth every twenty-nine days,
And every eight days, it will show a new phase."

Alonzo will grow through his phases and be
Unique as each rock that was shaped by the sea.

Alonzo is making slight changes with time,
So small he can't see them but someday he'll shine!

The year that he had with his teacher Ms. Crockett
Is when he sees changes speed up like a rocket.

Alonzo worked hard and he got his work done!
His third year of school went so fast and was fun!

If feelings of doubt in yourself
hold you back,

Believe in yourself, don't give up,
stay on track!

Be kind to yourself
and let time help you grow.

The Magic of Time will change you
more than you know.

www.ingramcontent.com/pod-product-compliance
Lightning Source LLC
LaVergne TN
LVHW072100070426
835508LV00002B/192